This book belongs to:

_____

For David, Angela, and Sara. I love you. - J.B.

Follow

@joanbangwrites

Copyright © 2021 by Joan Bang
All rights reserved. No part of this publication may be reproduced, stored in a retrieval system, or transmitted in any form or by any means, electronic, mechanical, photocopying, recording, or otherwise, without the prior permission of the publisher.

ISBN 978-1-7370860-0-0
Library of Congress Control Number 2021912921

THE Sea Otters WHO KEPT TRYING

by Joan Bang   illustrated by Teguh Sulistio

"Mama, tell us the story again!" said Oliver.
"Yes, the legend story!" Everly squealed.
"Okay," Mama agreed.

A long time ago, there was a family of sea otters who were trying to get a clam out of its shell to eat it.

Brother Otter said to his sister, "Use your teeth!"
She tried but she broke a tooth. "Waaa!" she cried.

Mother Otter suggested, "Try using your claws." Brother Otter tried but he broke one of his claws. **OUCH!**

An older otter swam by and shouted, "No one has ever been able to open a clam shell. Just give up."

Brother Otter said, "No, we won't give up! We can do it, right mama?"

"Like what?" wondered Brother Otter.
"This rock," said Mother Otter.

CRACK! CRUNCH!
She smashed the clam again and again until the shell opened and showed delicious gooey meat.
"We did it!" cheered Brother Otter.

The sea otter family shared their rock discovery with the other otters. Otters worldwide passed down the knowledge of how to open clams with a rock to each new generation.

"Sister Otter became legendary."

"What's legendary?" asked Everly.

"It's when you do something so amazing, it changes the world. It is thanks to Sister Otter that we can now easily enjoy delicious gooey clam meat. I have two special rocks that I want to give to each of you."

Mama handed Oliver and Everly each a rock.
"They look just like hearts!" said Everly.

"Yes, they are special," said Mama.
Oliver was curious, "What makes them special?"

"I searched high and low to find the perfect rock to give to you," Mama explained. "These two are special because they are heart-shaped and show my love for you."

"Use your new rocks to find lunch," said Mama. "I've been opening clams for you for a while. It's time for you to try on your own."

They dived into the water in search of clams and found some near a kelp forest.

Oliver flipped over onto his back and placed the rock on his tummy. Then, he smashed the clam against the rock. BAM! BAM! But the clam didn't open. He tried again. BAM! BAM! The clam still didn't open. "This isn't working," he whined.

"Let's keep trying," encouraged Everly. "I'll hold you still while you smash the clam."

Oliver placed the rock closer to his chest and smashed the clam against the rock again. BAM! BAM! He tried again. BAM! BAM! He tried again. CRACK! CRUNCH! The clam opened!

"Everly, we did it! Look at the meat. It's so gooey. Here, take a bite." beamed Oliver.

"Yum! That was tasty. We did it."

Fun Sea Otter Facts

- Sea otters have a loose pouch of skin that he or she uses to store food or a rock.

- Sea otters are one of the few mammal species to use tools.

- A baby sea otter is called a pup.

- A mother sea otter sometimes wraps her pup with kelp to keep him or her from floating away.

- A group of floating sea otters is called a raft.

- Sea otters sometimes hold paws when they sleep to keep from drifting apart.

- Sea otter fur is the densest of any mammal at about 1 million hairs per square inch.

CPSIA information can be obtained
at www.ICGtesting.com
Printed in the USA
BVHW020847070821
613729BV00007BA/783